THE LITTLE BOOK OF
RETIREMENT

THE LITTLE BOOK OF RETIREMENT

Copyright © Summersdale Publishers Ltd, 2016

Text contributed by Clive Whichelow

An Hachette UK Company
www.hachette.co.uk

Summersdale Publishers Ltd
Part of Octopus Publishing Group Limited
Carmelite House
50 Victoria Embankment
LONDON
EC4Y 0DZ
UK

www.summersdale.com

Printed and bound in Malta

ISBN: 978-1-84953-851-0

Substantial discounts on bulk quantities of Summersdale books are available to corporations, professional associations and other organisations. For details contact general enquiries: telephone: +44 (0) 1243 771107 or email: enquiries@summersdale.com.

THE LITTLE BOOK OF
RETIREMENT

FREDDIE GREEN

summersdale

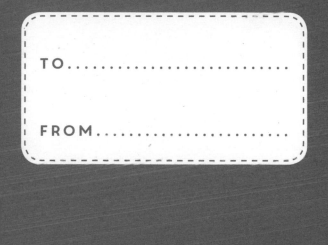

TO..............................

FROM..............................

THE GOLDEN AGE
IS BEFORE US, NOT
BEHIND US.

Sallust

THERE IS A WHOLE NEW KIND OF LIFE AHEAD... SOME CALL IT RETIREMENT. I CALL IT BLISS.

Betty Sullivan

YOUR IDEA OF EARLY RISING IS 10.00 A.M. – AND EVEN THEN IT'S A STRUGGLE.

LIFE IS A PROGRESS
AND NOT A STATION.

Ralph Waldo Emerson

HOW BEAUTIFUL IT IS TO DO NOTHING AND THEN REST AFTERWARDS.

Spanish proverb

YOU KNOW YOU'RE RETIRED WHEN...

**YOU HAVE TO START
BUYING YOUR
OWN STATIONERY
– A PACKET OF
ENVELOPES COSTS
HOW MUCH?!**

AGE IS JUST A NUMBER.
IT'S TOTALLY IRRELEVANT
UNLESS, OF COURSE,
YOU HAPPEN TO BE A
BOTTLE OF WINE.

Joan Collins

YOUR BODY CLOCK STILL WAKES YOU AT THE CRACK OF DAWN, WHICH IS QUITE ANNOYING NOW THAT YOU DON'T HAVE TO BE ANYWHERE IN PARTICULAR.

YOU CAN HAVE A
'CAKE FRIDAY' ALL
TO YOURSELF – YOU
GREEDY THING!

AGEING IS NOT 'LOST YOUTH' BUT A NEW STAGE OF OPPORTUNITY AND STRENGTH.

Betty Friedan

RETIREMENT AT 65 IS RIDICULOUS. WHEN I WAS 65 I STILL HAD PIMPLES.

George Burns

**YOU THROW DARTS
AT A DARTBOARD
RATHER THAN
AT A PHOTO OF
YOUR BOSS.**

YOU CAN'T HAVE A 'QUICK PINT' ON THE WAY HOME ANY MORE.

DON'T LET AGEING GET YOU DOWN. IT'S TOO HARD TO GET BACK UP.

John Wagner

TRAVEL AND CHANGE OF PLACE IMPART NEW VIGOUR TO THE MIND.

Seneca the Younger

OLD AGE HAS ITS PLEASURES, WHICH, THOUGH DIFFERENT, ARE NOT LESS THAN THE PLEASURES OF YOUTH.

W. Somerset Maugham

**YOU GET ON
TRAINS AND BUSES
AND THERE ARE
SEATS AVAILABLE
– HURRAH!**

I DON'T WANT TO RETIRE.
I'M NOT THAT GOOD AT
CROSSWORD PUZZLES.

Norman Mailer

YOUTH IS THE GIFT
OF NATURE, BUT AGE
IS A WORK OF ART.

Garson Kanin

YOU WONDER
HOW YOU EVER
FOUND THE TIME
TO GO TO WORK.

LIFE HAS GOT TO BE LIVED – THAT'S ALL THERE IS TO IT.

Eleanor Roosevelt

YOU CAN HAVE A HOLIDAY WITHOUT CHECKING THE DATES WITH ANYONE ELSE!

PUTTING YOUR FEET
UP IS NO LONGER
A NOVELTY.

**HALF OUR LIFE IS
SPENT TRYING TO FIND
SOMETHING TO DO
WITH THE TIME WE HAVE
RUSHED THROUGH LIFE
TRYING TO SAVE.**

Will Rogers

THE ROLE OF A RETIRED PERSON IS NO LONGER TO HAVE ONE.

Simone de Beauvoir

YOU'VE REDISCOVERED THE ART OF MOOCHING ABOUT, WHICH HAS LAIN DORMANT SINCE YOUR TEENAGE YEARS.

YOU REALISE YOU
HAVEN'T WOUND
YOUR ALARM CLOCK
FOR SIX MONTHS.

MY IDEA OF HELL IS TO
BE YOUNG AGAIN.

Marge Piercy

**WORKING PEOPLE HAVE
A LOT OF BAD HABITS,
BUT THE WORST OF
THEM IS WORK.**

Clarence Darrow

I NEVER RETIRED. I JUST DID SOMETHING ELSE.

Doris Day

YOU SMILE WRYLY
AS YOU REMEMBER
THAT ALL YOUR
OLD COLLEAGUES
ARE STILL HARD AT
IT WHILE YOU'RE
HAVING A LONG
SOAK IN THE BATH.

A LIFE WHICH IS EMPTY OF PURPOSE UNTIL 65 WILL NOT SUDDENLY BECOME FILLED ON RETIREMENT.

Dwight L. Moody

WE DO NOT STOP PLAYING BECAUSE WE GROW OLD. WE GROW OLD BECAUSE WE STOP PLAYING.

G. Stanley Hall

SOMEHOW IT'S NOT
AS MUCH FUN TO BE
WASTING YOUR OWN
TIME INSTEAD OF
SOMEONE ELSE'S.

DO NOT WORRY ABOUT AVOIDING TEMPTATION. AS YOU GROW OLDER IT WILL AVOID YOU.

Anonymous

YOU KNOW YOU'RE RETIRED WHEN...

**TIME SEEMS TO
FLY BY NOW THAT
YOU'RE NOT CLOCK-
WATCHING ALL DAY.**

YOUR GARDEN IS
NOW THE NEATEST
IN THE STREET.

WHAT DO GARDENERS DO
WHEN THEY RETIRE?

Bob Monkhouse

TOO MANY PEOPLE...
THINK THAT THEY HAVE TO
LIVE BY THE CALENDAR.

John Glenn

ALL YOUR WORK-AVOIDANCE SCHEMES HAVE BECOME REDUNDANT – UNTIL YOUR PARTNER FINDS 'A LITTLE JOB' FOR YOU.

EVERY DAY IS DRESS-DOWN FRIDAY – THOUGH PYJAMAS AT LUNCHTIME MIGHT BE PUSHING IT A BIT, ESPECIALLY IF YOU'RE IN THE LOCAL CAFE.

AGE IS NOT A PARTICULARLY INTERESTING SUBJECT. ANYONE CAN GET OLD. ALL YOU HAVE TO DO IS LIVE LONG ENOUGH.

Groucho Marx

IF PEOPLE CONCENTRATED
ON THE REALLY IMPORTANT
THINGS IN LIFE, THERE'D
BE A SHORTAGE OF
FISHING POLES.

Doug Larson

THE OLDER I GET, THE BETTER I USED TO BE.

John McEnroe

**YOU REALISE THAT
YOU HAVEN'T HEARD
ANY GOOD GOSSIP
FOR MONTHS.**

THE YEARS BETWEEN 50
AND 70 ARE THE HARDEST.
YOU ARE ALWAYS
ASKED TO DO THINGS,
AND YET YOU ARE NOT
DECREPIT ENOUGH TO
TURN THEM DOWN.

T. S. Eliot

THE BEST TIME TO START THINKING ABOUT YOUR RETIREMENT IS BEFORE THE BOSS DOES.

Anonymous

FLICKING RUBBER
BANDS AND PLAYING
SOLITAIRE ON
THE COMPUTER
JUST DON'T HOLD
THE APPEAL THEY
ONCE DID.

CESSATION OF WORK IS NOT ACCOMPANIED BY CESSATION OF EXPENSES.

Cato the Elder

YOU HAVE TO TRUDGE AROUND TOWN TO FIND A PRINT/COPY SHOP WHEN YOU NEED TO PRINT SOMETHING.

YOU KNOW YOU'RE RETIRED WHEN...

YOU DON'T HAVE A
WHOLE BUNCH OF
PEOPLE TO DISCUSS
LAST NIGHT'S TV
WITH – THE BUDGIE
DOESN'T COUNT.

YOUTH WOULD BE AN IDEAL STATE IF IT CAME A LITTLE LATER IN LIFE.

H. H. Asquith

I'M NOW AS FREE AS THE BREEZE – WITH ROUGHLY THE SAME INCOME.

Gene Perret

EVERYONE ELSE IN THE STREET SEES YOU AS AN UNPAID DOG WALKER AND HOUSE-SITTER.

YOU CAN SPEND AN
ENTIRE MORNING
TRYING TO DECIDE
WHAT TO HAVE
FOR LUNCH.

HOW PLEASANT IS THE
DAY WHEN WE GIVE
UP STRIVING TO BE
YOUNG – OR SLENDER.

William James

**RETIREMENT CAN BE A
GREAT JOY IF YOU CAN
FIGURE OUT HOW TO
SPEND TIME WITHOUT
SPENDING MONEY.**

Anonymous

WHEN A MAN RETIRES, HIS WIFE GETS TWICE THE HUSBAND BUT ONLY HALF THE INCOME.

Chi Chi Rodriguez

**BEFORE LONG,
YOU'VE COMPLETELY
FORGOTTEN WHAT
IT IS THAT YOU
USED TO DO.**

LOOKING 50 IS GREAT
– IF YOU'RE 60.

Joan Rivers

LEARN FROM YESTERDAY, LIVE FOR TODAY, HOPE FOR TOMORROW. THE IMPORTANT THING IS NOT TO STOP QUESTIONING.

Albert Einstein

YOU CAN'T RESIST
WALKING PAST YOUR
OLD WORKPLACE
TO SEE HOW IT'S
ALL GONE TO POT
SINCE YOU LEFT.

YOU DON'T GET OLDER,
YOU GET BETTER.

Shirley Bassey

YOU'RE FILLING IN AN OFFICIAL FORM AND YOU'RE STUMPED AS TO WHAT TO WRITE UNDER 'OCCUPATION'.

YOU KNOW YOU'RE RETIRED WHEN...

YOU CAN'T REMEMBER WHAT IT'S LIKE TO GO OUT IN THE DARK MORNINGS – THANK GOODNESS!

MUSICIANS DON'T RETIRE; THEY STOP WHEN THERE'S NO MORE MUSIC IN THEM.

Louis Armstrong

RETIREMENT IS WONDERFUL IF YOU HAVE TWO ESSENTIALS – MUCH TO LIVE ON AND MUCH TO LIVE FOR.

Anonymous

**YOU WONDER
IF THERE'S ANY
WAY TO AVOID
TAKING UP GOLF.**

YOU WISH YOU'D
GOT ONE OF THOSE
JOBS WHERE YOU
RETIRE AT 45.

THE SECRET OF STAYING YOUNG IS TO LIVE HONESTLY, EAT SLOWLY AND LIE ABOUT YOUR AGE.

Lucille Ball

WHEN YOU'VE BEEN LIVING IN THE SUNSHINE ALL YOUR LIFE, YOU DON'T WANT TO MOVE INTO THE SHADE.

Don Hewitt

AGE IS ONLY A NUMBER,
A CIPHER FOR THE
RECORDS. EXPERIENCE
ACHIEVES MORE WITH
LESS ENERGY AND TIME.

Bernard Baruch

YOU TAKE A SUDDEN,
KEEN INTEREST IN
RESEARCHING YOUR
FAMILY TREE.

LIFE BEGINS AT
RETIREMENT.

Anonymous

THE PROBLEM OF AGEING IS THE PROBLEM OF LIVING. THERE IS NO SIMPLE SOLUTION.

Coco Chanel

YOU SERIOUSLY
CONSIDER PUTTING
A TIME LOCK ON THE
FRIDGE TO KEEP YOU
FROM TEMPTATION.

I HAVE NEVER LIKED WORKING. TO ME A JOB IS AN INVASION OF PRIVACY.

Danny McGoorty

YOU WONDER
WHETHER IT WAS
WISE TO HAVE
CASHED IN HALF
YOUR SAVINGS TO
FUND A HOLIDAY
WHEN YOU WERE 35.

YOU'RE DELIGHTED
TO FIND THAT THE
ROADS AREN'T
GRIDLOCKED ALL
DAY LONG AND
THAT YOU CAN
EVEN GO OVER
8 MPH AT TIMES.

IT'S SAD TO GROW OLD,
BUT NICE TO RIPEN.

Brigitte Bardot

YOUTHFULNESS IS ABOUT HOW YOU LIVE, NOT WHEN YOU WERE BORN.

Karl Lagerfeld

ALL YOUR FRIENDS
KEEP ASKING,
'WHAT DO YOU DO
WITH YOURSELF ALL
DAY?' AND YOU'RE
HONESTLY NOT SURE
HOW TO REPLY.

INSTEAD OF DOING A WEEKLY GROCERY SHOP, YOU'RE POPPING OUT SIX TIMES A DAY FOR 'THIS AND THAT' AND YOU'RE ON FIRST-NAME TERMS WITH ALL THE SUPERMARKET STAFF.

I AM GETTING TO AN AGE
WHEN I CAN ONLY ENJOY
THE LAST SPORT LEFT. IT
IS CALLED HUNTING FOR
YOUR SPECTACLES.

Edward Grey

**THE QUESTION ISN'T
AT WHAT AGE I WANT
TO RETIRE, IT'S AT
WHAT INCOME.**

George Foreman

GOLF IS A DAY SPENT IN A ROUND OF STRENUOUS IDLENESS.

William Wordsworth

RATHER THAN WORKING ALL DAY WITH THE OCCASIONAL TEA BREAK, YOU HAVE ONE LONG TEA-DRINKING SESSION WITH THE ODD WORK BREAK (IF YOU CAN CALL A WORD SEARCH PUZZLE 'WORK').

IF YOU WAIT, ALL
THAT HAPPENS IS THAT
YOU GET OLDER.

Larry McMurtry

GROW OLD ALONG WITH ME! THE BEST IS YET TO BE.

Robert Browning

FOR THE FIRST TIME EVER, YOU'RE AT HOME WHEN THE METER READER AND POSTMAN CALL, SO THERE'S NO NEED FOR THEM TO LEAVE THOSE ANNOYING *SORRY, YOU WERE OUT* CARDS.

YOU ONLY LIVE ONCE, BUT IF YOU DO IT RIGHT, ONCE IS ENOUGH.

Mae West

YOU HAVE NO EXCUSE TO PUT OFF ALL THOSE DIY AND DECORATING JOBS THAT HAVE BEEN PILING UP FOR YEARS.

YOU'RE OFFICIALLY
NOTHING TO DO
WITH THE STATE OF
THE ECONOMY BUT
YOU GIVE ADVICE
TO ALL AND SUNDRY
ON HOW IT SHOULD
BE IMPROVED.

**THERE ARE SOME WHO
START THEIR RETIREMENT
LONG BEFORE THEY
STOP WORKING.**

Anonymous

TO LIVE IS A
WONDERFUL THING.

Coco Chanel

YOU NO LONGER
HAVE TO CHECK
YOUR DIARY
WHEN MAKING
APPOINTMENTS AS
YOU'RE GENERALLY
AVAILABLE.

YOU'RE THE GO-TO
PERSON FOR THE
REST OF THE FAMILY
FOR PICKING UP
THE DRY-CLEANING
AND RETURNING
LIBRARY BOOKS.

MEN FOR THE SAKE OF GETTING A LIVING FORGET TO LIVE.

Margaret Fuller

YOU CAN'T TURN BACK THE CLOCK, BUT YOU CAN WIND IT UP AGAIN.

Bonnie Prudden

RETIRE FROM WORK,
BUT NOT FROM LIFE.

Anonymous

IT'S ALWAYS YOUR
TURN TO MAKE THE
TEA NOWADAYS.

WHEN THEY TELL ME I'M TOO OLD TO DO SOMETHING, I ATTEMPT IT IMMEDIATELY.

Pablo Picasso

DON'T SIMPLY RETIRE FROM SOMETHING; HAVE SOMETHING TO RETIRE TO.

Harry Emerson Fosdick

YOU KNOW YOU'RE RETIRED WHEN...

YOU HAVE TO FIND
THINGS TO OCCUPY
YOU DURING THE
DAY – JUST LIKE AT
WORK REALLY.

**PEOPLE ARE ALWAYS
ASKING ABOUT THE
GOOD OLD DAYS. I SAY,
WHY DON'T YOU SAY
THE GOOD NOW DAYS?**

Robert M. Young

NO ONE CAN TELL
YOU WHAT TO DO
ANY MORE – APART
FROM YOUR OTHER
HALF, OF COURSE.

YOU KNOW YOU'RE RETIRED WHEN...

PEOPLE FROM WORK
KEEP PHONING UP
ASKING WHERE
ON EARTH YOU
PUT IMPORTANT
DOCUMENTS.

DON'T PLAY TOO MUCH GOLF. TWO ROUNDS A DAY ARE PLENTY.

Harry Vardon

I'M NOT INTERESTED
IN AGE. PEOPLE WHO
TELL ME THEIR AGE
ARE SILLY. YOU'RE AS
OLD AS YOU FEEL.

Elizabeth Arden

YOU'RE RELIEVED
YOU DON'T HAVE
TO GET USED TO
THE OFFICE'S
NEWFANGLED
IT SYSTEM.

YOU NO LONGER
CARE WHAT THE
WEATHER WILL BE
DOING TODAY AS
YOU CAN STAY AT
HOME. HURRICANES,
BLIZZARDS?
BRING 'EM ON!

RETIREMENT: THE WORLD'S LONGEST COFFEE BREAK.

Anonymous

OLD AGE AIN'T NO
PLACE FOR SISSIES.

Bette Davis

**OLD PEOPLE SHOULDN'T
EAT HEALTH FOODS.
THEY NEED ALL THE
PRESERVATIVES
THEY CAN GET.**

Robert Orben

**YOU FINALLY
FIND OUT WHY
EVERYONE MOANS
ABOUT THE STATE
OF DAYTIME TV.**

THE KEY TO SUCCESSFUL AGEING IS TO PAY AS LITTLE ATTENTION TO IT AS POSSIBLE.

Judith Regan

THE BEST IS ALWAYS
YET TO COME.

Lucy Larcom

AT LAST YOU CAN
WRITE YOUR NOVEL,
LEARN A MUSICAL
INSTRUMENT
AND GO ON THAT
WORLD CRUISE –
THOUGH MAYBE
NOT ALL AT ONCE.

YOU ARE ONLY YOUNG ONCE, BUT YOU CAN STAY IMMATURE INDEFINITELY.

Ogden Nash

**YOU'VE BECOME
A REGULAR ON
RADIO PHONE-INS.**

YOUR
OPPORTUNITIES FOR
OFFICE ROMANCE
ARE NOW ZERO.

**NOBODY CAN GO BACK
AND START A NEW
BEGINNING, BUT ANYONE
CAN START TODAY AND
MAKE A NEW ENDING.**

Maria Robinson

THE TROUBLE WITH RETIREMENT IS THAT YOU NEVER GET A DAY OFF.

Abe Lemons

**YOU CAN CATCH
JUNK MAILERS
RED-HANDED.**

YOU'VE BEEN PROMOTED TO HEAD OF YOUR LOCAL NEIGHBOURHOOD WATCH AND HAVE PERFECTED YOUR CURTAIN-TWITCHING SKILLS.

I ENJOY WAKING UP AND
NOT HAVING TO GO TO
WORK. SO I DO IT THREE
OR FOUR TIMES A DAY.

Gene Perret

MAY YOU LIVE AS LONG AS YOU WANT, AND NEVER WANT AS LONG AS YOU LIVE.

Irish blessing

GROWING OLD IS COMPULSORY. GROWING UP IS OPTIONAL.

Bob Monkhouse

**YOUR CLOTHES
SEEM TO BE A BIT
TIGHTER, STRANGE...**

THE FUTURE BELONGS TO THOSE WHO BELIEVE IN THE BEAUTY OF THEIR DREAMS.

Eleanor Roosevelt

WHEN A MAN RETIRES AND TIME IS NO LONGER A MATTER OF URGENT IMPORTANCE, HIS COLLEAGUES GENERALLY PRESENT HIM WITH A WATCH.

R. C. Sherriff

ALL THE DOUBLE-GLAZING SALESMEN HAVE STOPPED CALLING BECAUSE YOU'VE BEEN AT HOME TO TELL THEM TO GET LOST SO MANY TIMES.

I'M RETIRED.
GOODBYE, TENSION.
HELLO, PENSION!

Anonymous

**YOU'VE BECOME
AN EXPERT ON
ALL THE DAILY
CROSSWORDS AND
SUDOKU PUZZLES.**

YOU STILL GO TO THE
PUB EVERY FRIDAY
AT 5.30 P.M. OUT
OF PURE HABIT.

DON'T LIVE THE SAME YEAR 75 TIMES AND CALL IT A LIFE.

Robin Sharma

A COMFORTABLE OLD AGE IS THE REWARD OF A WELL-SPENT YOUTH.

Maurice Chevalier

SUDDENLY ALL THE PEOPLE YOU SOCIALISE WITH DURING THE DAY ARE RELATIVELY OLD.

YOU CAN
CEREMONIALLY
BURN YOUR CV.

YOU CAN'T HELP GETTING OLDER, BUT YOU DON'T HAVE TO GET OLD.

George Burns

RETIREMENT BRINGS
REPOSE, AND REPOSE
ALLOWS A KINDLY
JUDGEMENT OF
ALL THINGS.

John Sharp Williams

I HAVE FOUND THAT IF YOU LOVE LIFE, LIFE WILL LOVE YOU BACK.

Arthur Rubinstein

YOU'RE SAVING A
SMALL FORTUNE
ON LEAVING
COLLECTIONS.

RETIREMENT IS WHEN YOU STOP LIVING AT WORK AND BEGIN WORKING AT LIVING.

Anonymous

HE WHO IS OF A CALM AND HAPPY NATURE WILL HARDLY FEEL THE PRESSURE OF AGE.

Plato

IT'S NO BIG DEAL
TO HAVE A LIE-IN
AT THE WEEKEND –
OR ANY OTHER DAY,
FOR THAT MATTER!

TO GET BACK MY YOUTH
I WOULD DO ANYTHING IN
THE WORLD, EXCEPT TAKE
EXERCISE, GET UP EARLY,
OR BE RESPECTABLE.

Oscar Wilde

YOU KNOW YOU'RE RETIRED WHEN...

AT LAST YOU CAN
STOP PAYING INTO
YOUR PENSION!

THE MONEY'S NO BETTER
IN RETIREMENT BUT
THE HOURS ARE!

Terri Guillemets

TO KEEP THE HEART UNWRINKLED, TO BE HOPEFUL, KINDLY, CHEERFUL, REVERENT – THAT IS TO TRIUMPH OVER OLD AGE.

Thomas Bailey Aldrich

WISH NOT SO MUCH
TO LIVE LONG AS
TO LIVE WELL.

Benjamin Franklin

CUSTOMERS IN
CHARITY SHOPS
ASSUME THAT
YOU'RE ONE OF
THE STAFF.

THE IMPORTANT THING IS NOT HOW MANY YEARS IN YOUR LIFE BUT HOW MUCH LIFE IN YOUR YEARS.

Edward Stieglitz

MAY YOU LIVE ALL THE DAYS OF YOUR LIFE.

Jonathan Swift

If you're interested in finding
out more about our books,
find us on Facebook at
SUMMERSDALE PUBLISHERS
and follow us on Twitter at
@SUMMERSDALE.

WWW.SUMMERSDALE.COM